AZTEC
TECHNOLOGY AND ART

HISTORY 4TH GRADE
Children's History Books

BABY PROFESSOR
EDUCATION KIDS

Speedy Publishing LLC
40 E. Main St. #1156
Newark, DE 19711
www.speedypublishing.com
Copyright 2017

All Rights reserved. No part of this book may be reproduced or used in any way or form or by any means whether electronic or mechanical, this means that you cannot record or photocopy any material ideas or tips that are provided in this book.

The Aztec Empire made great discoveries in ways of telling time, in medicine, in weapons, and in fine art. Let's find out what they were up to.

A WORLD OF WAR

The Aztecs are most famous for being an empire always at war, always fighting its neighbors, and for ceremonies that involved human sacrifices to please their gods. But the six million people of the empire were up to a lot more than just fighting.

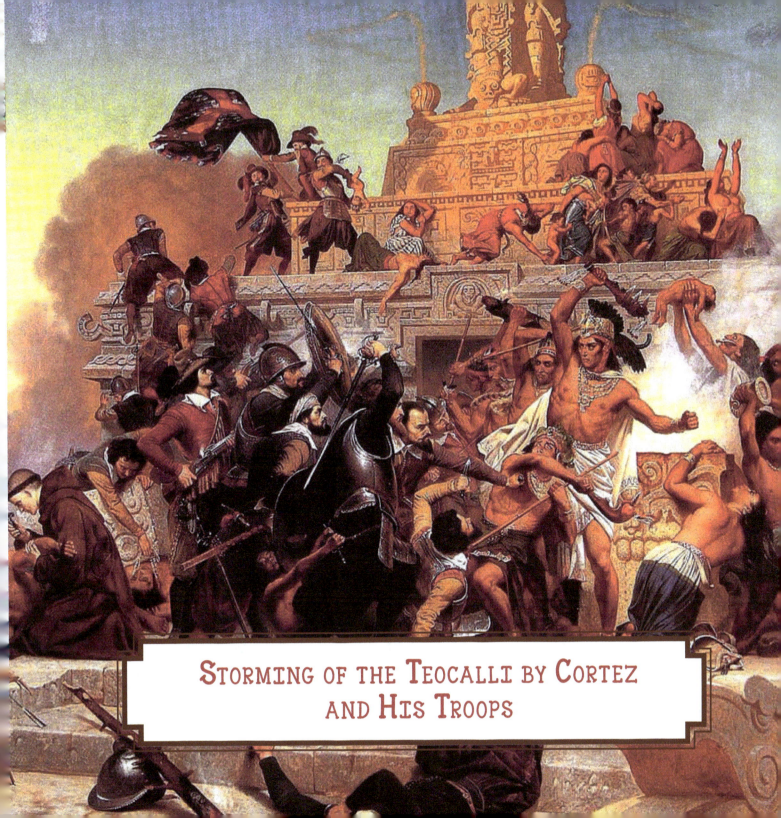

Storming of the Teocalli by Cortez and His Troops

STORMING OF THE TEOCALLI BY CORTEZ AND HIS TROOPS

The Aztecs were required to fight to make a place for themselves. When they arrived in the area around what is now Mexico City, around 1250 CE, the land was already occupied. There were many other cultures, and none of them welcomed the newcomers. The Aztecs could barely find land on which to grow crops.

Finally the Aztecs started building their great city, Tenochtitlan, on an island in Lake Texcoco, in 1325. While they built the city, they had to keep fighting the other city-states nearby. Only in 1430, when the Aztecs allied with two other large cities, did they become a dominant force in the area.

THE BATTLE OF AZCAPOTZALCO

The Aztec Empire grew through fighting, absorbing other cities and peoples, until 1521. Then invaders from Europe arrived and the empire came to an end. Read about that in the Baby Professor book The Spanish Conquistadors Conquer the Aztecs.

Aztec sacrificial knives

TECHNOLOGY

The Aztecs did not develop the ability to make tools or weapons from iron or bronze. They had to combine other materials, like wood, bone, and stone. Many of their weapons had cutting edges made of obsidian, a glass-like rock created by volcanic eruptions.

When the Europeans appeared in the early sixteenth century, the Aztecs were starting to use weapons and tools with copper cutting edges, or a combination of stone and copper. They were inventive, making drills out of bone or reeds.

Spear hrads

Spears and Atlatls

TECHNOLOGY FOR WAR

WEAPONS

The Aztecs developed a wide range of weapons. They invented:

- The atlatl, which let the user throw a spear or a dart further and with more power. They could use this for fishing and hunting as well as for war.

- The **macuahuitl**, a wooden club with obsidian blades in its head. They used this weapon to hurt an enemy but not kill him, because they often wanted to capture enemy fighters to use in human sacrifices.

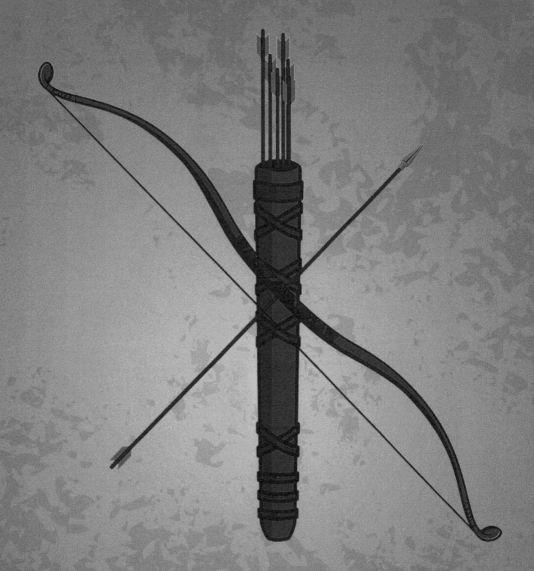

- They developed bows and arrows that were similar to those developed in Europe, Africa, and Asia.

ARMOR

The Aztecs did not have iron to make armor with, so their fighters never had as much protection as a European knight did. They also did not have horses that a knight needed to ride into battle.

The Aztecs used shields made of wood or woven reeds, and then covered with leather to make them tougher. The leather covers were often decorated with designs, or pictures of birds or even butterflies.

Helmets: The best warriors sometimes wore leather helmets that had designs to show their rank and what part of the army they belonged to.

Body armor: Some fighters wore ichcahuipilli, quilted cotton tunics, to protect their bodies. The tunics were made stiffer by being soaked in salt water.

UNIFORMS

The Aztec fighters did not have a uniform the way European armies did, but different classes of fighters dressed differently:

- Ordinary fighters wore a tunic or an ichcahuipilli and decorated themselves with paint.

- Expert fighters added feathers and animal skins to make themselves look more impressive.

- A jaguar fighter could wear a whole jaguar skin and a helmet with jaguar fangs attached to it.
- Eagle fighters had suits made of feathers, decorated with eagle talons, and helmets with beaks.

JAGUAR FIGHTER

TRANSPORTATION

The Aztecs knew about the wheel, but they only used it for children's toys. They had no large animals that could pull wagons over long distances, and so never developed the sort of wheeled carts, wagons, and chariots that other cultures developed.

To carry goods long distances, Aztecs used dugout canoes. They created a system of canals joining rivers and lakes so their canoes could travel throughout the Aztec Empire.

MEDICINE

The Aztecs developed many medicines to deal with common human problems, and studied plants to learn how they might be used to heal people who were sick. A document from 1552, the Badianus Manuscript, is a beautiful illustrated guide to a wide range of plants, describing how to use them to prepare medicine, and what problems the medicine would address.

SCIENCE AND NUMBERS

The Aztecs were good mathematicians and careful scientists. Their number system was very advanced. They knew a lot about astronomy and had detailed maps of the stars, because this knowledge connected to their calendar and to their worship of their many gods.

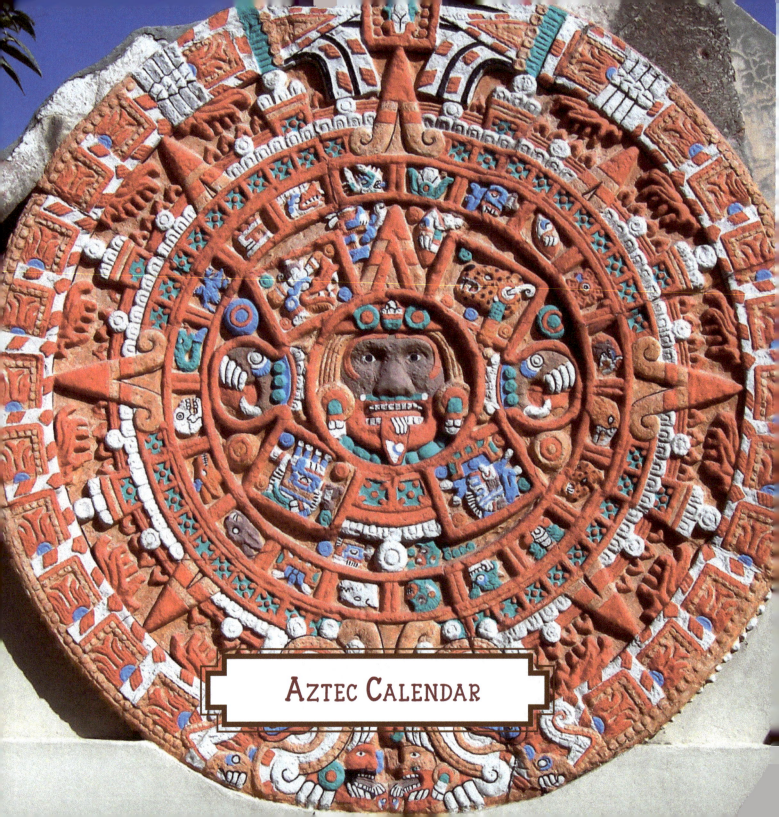
Aztec Calendar

THE AZTEC CALENDARS

The Aztecs developed two detailed and complex calendars which served different purposes in their religion and culture. The xiuhpohualli was a calendar for a 365-day year. It marked the seasons, important civic events, and when planting, harvesting and other events should start or take place. This was like the calendar we are familiar with.

The **tonalpohualli** was a 260-day calendar. The name means "the count of days", and it was the calendar which tracked and marked religious events. Physically, this calendar marked 20 weeks, each of thirteen days.

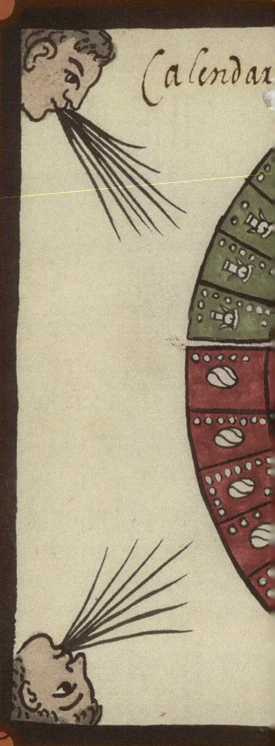

Aztec ritual for flooding

For the Aztecs, it was essential to celebrate religious rituals on the correct days, and the tonalpohualli showed what should happen, and when. Without the rituals, the Aztecs believed, the world would fall into chaos.

Aztec ritual for flooding

They believed that the gods were involved in a constant battle against the forces of evil and darkness, and that humans could help the gods by offering sacrifices on the correct days. Each day in the tonalpohualli was dedicated to the god or force of nature that gave the world and its people energy on that day.

ART

The art of the Aztec Empire developed from the art and culture of the many tribes and peoples that were part of the empire. Some of the patterns of art were thousands of years old. In fact, the Aztec word for works of art was "toltecat". This came from the name of the Toltec tribe, whose city had huge statues of Toltec gods. The city was destroyed in the twelfth century, but the statues remained and impressed the Aztecs.

TOLTECA

Works of art were made for, and kept by, the leading members of the empire. Ordinary people did not hang pictures on their walls or have complicated jewelry.

However, the empire did trade works of art with other empires and city-states, and imported art and the raw materials to make fine works from other societies.

TULA

Much of the art is a celebration of nature. There are pictures of plants and animals from the Aztec world—aloe plants, ducks, monkeys, snakes, palm trees, and dogs, among other subjects. Sometimes the pictures show Aztec fighters dressed for battle, captive soldiers, or victims being sacrificed to the gods.

A lot of the art is related to the worship of the hundreds of gods the Aztecs believed governed the world and their lives. The images of the gods have bright colors and sharp angles.

CLOTHING

The upper class of the Aztec Empire had complex and beautiful clothing. A lot of it was decorated with silver, jewels, and feathers. The emperor had a crown, or headdress, of green feathers with blue and gold threads holding them together. The ruling families wore necklaces, earrings, and bracelets that were made of the most expensive materials.

STORY-TELLING

Scrolls and wall paintings that told stories of great events, or described the gods, or showed scenes of everyday life, were usually full of pictures, like a graphic novel. The pictures are bright and complicated.

The Red Jaguar mural

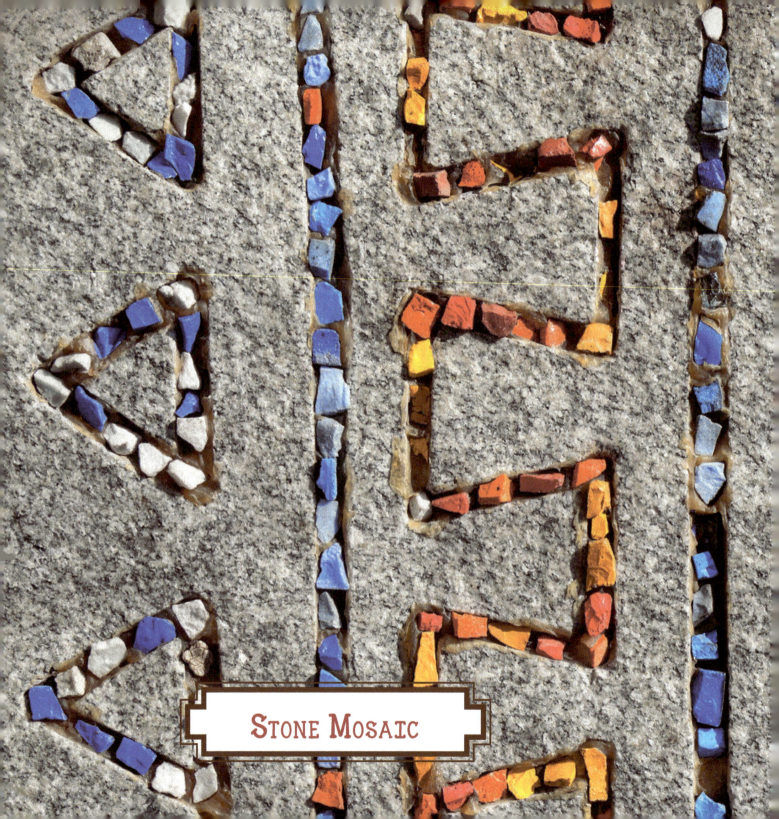

MOSAICS

The Aztecs used mosaics, building up an image with many small bits of colored stone, to decorate masks, the clothing for rituals, and walls of buildings. The artists used bits of turquoise and of crushed shells to add texture and color.

STONE ART

Artists worked in stone to create a wide range of beautiful products, from shaped pillars that decorated buildings to pottery that was used both for everyday cooking and in special ceremonies. Many weapons were made of stone, as were parts of some shields.

Handmade Ethnic Clay Beaded Jewelry

OTHER MATERIALS

Beside stone, the Aztecs used copper, jewels, gold, silver, feathers, and clay in their art. They traded with other cultures for the raw materials they could not find locally.

STYLE

Statues of people and of gods were very lifelike. In many of the statues you can see the marks of battle or the signs of age and struggle: these are not imaginary creatures, but realistic renderings of real people. Even the animals and trees are very realistic, and show that the artists paid close attention to the subjects of their work.

Detail of the temple of Quetzalcoatl

A lot of the art is about struggle, battle, victory, and death. The world was not a peaceful place for the Aztecs, and their art reflects the struggle they felt all around them.

There is so much to learn about the Aztecs. Its civilization was complicated and interesting. The Aztecs worshipped hundreds of gods. They have their unique way of governance. Find out more about Aztec Government and Society, their many gods and how wonderful their technology and art was.

Learn more by reading other Baby Professor books about the Aztecs and searching the website of your favorite book retailer.

Milton Keynes UK
Ingram Content Group UK Ltd.
UKHW051123030924
447802UK00003B/39